Nocturnes for piano

No.1 ÷ 2

from the music cycle
" PLAY OF THE THOUGHT "

Hristo Tsanov

ISBN-13: 978-1544145020
ISBN-10: 1544145020

CONTENTS:

Hristo Tsanov

4

Nocturno for piano No.1

from the music cycle " PLAY OF THE THOUGHT "

Nocturno for piano No.1

10

A Tempo I. Moderato espressivo
ad lib.
A Tempo I. Andante a carezzevole
poco a poco accel.

33
8va
ad lib.
a tempo
8va
8va
ff
ff
f
p
f
f
8va
8vb
38
8va
8vb
p
8va
f
40
8va
8va
8va
p
f
42
Piu mosso affannoso
8va
8va
7
16
7
16
p
8va
45

8

Pesante
A Tempo I.
Pesante
A Tempo I.

70
74
Pesante
C
ff
CADENZA
Tempo ad libitum
10
16
p
78
80
82

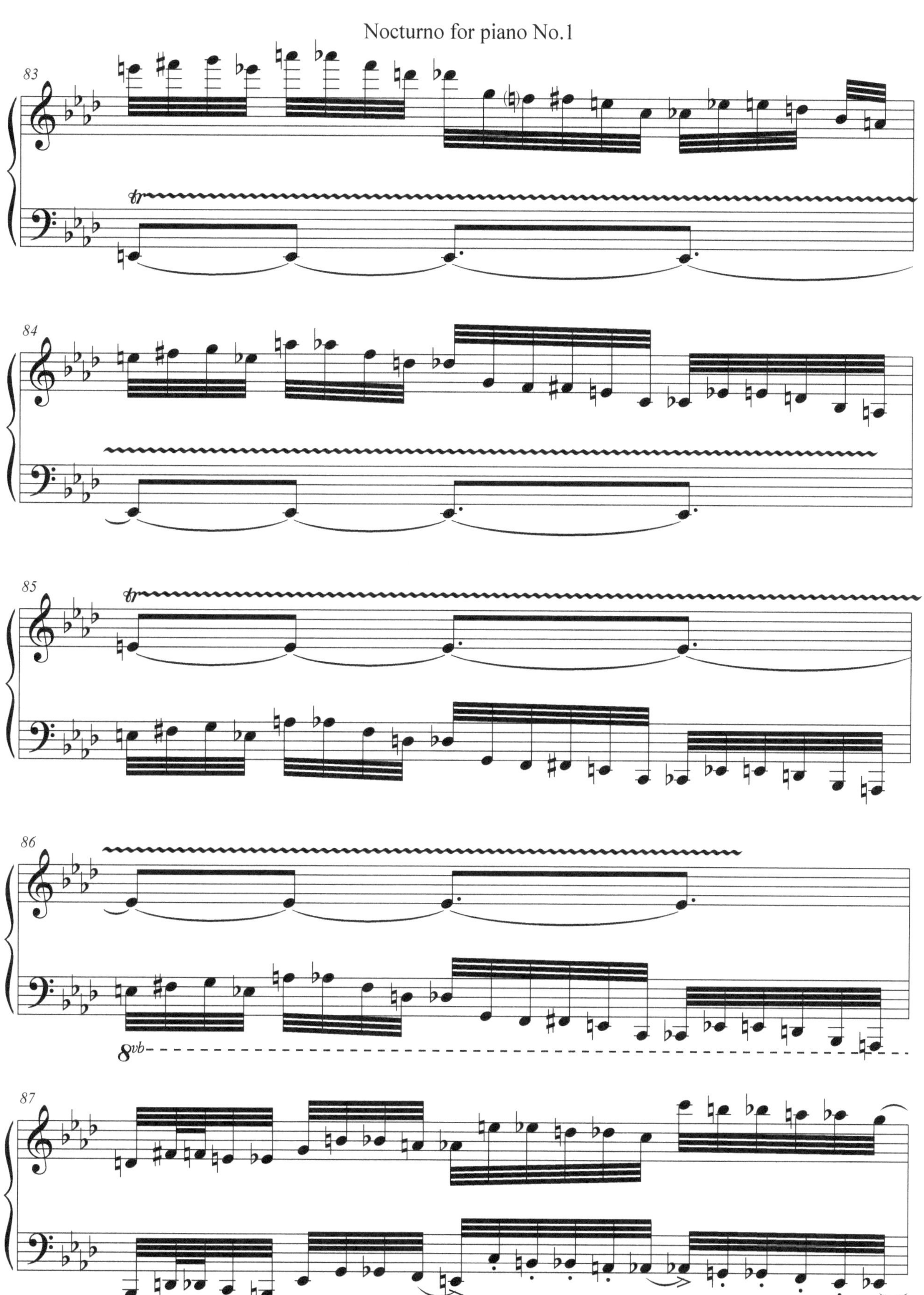

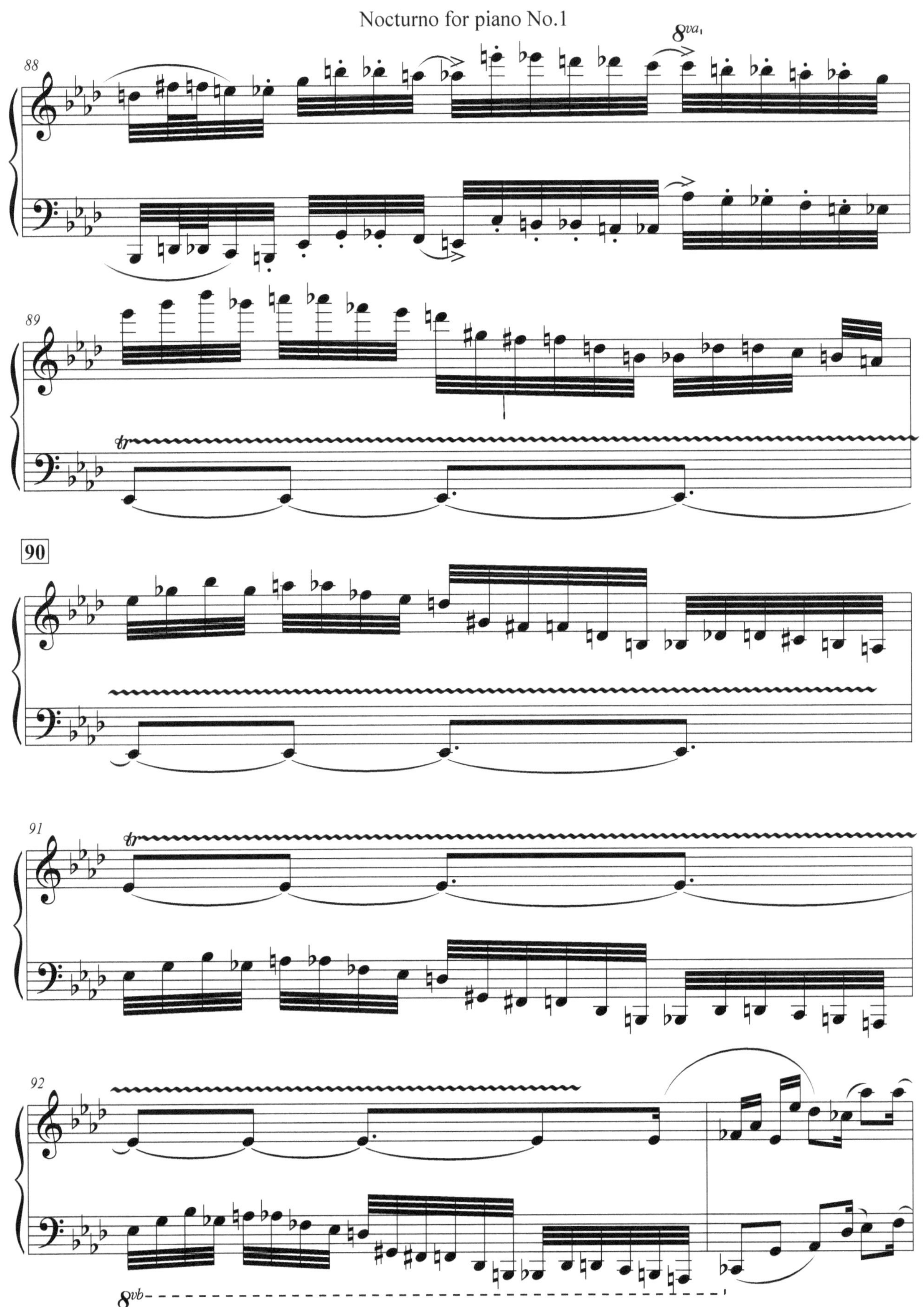
Nocturno for piano No.1

Nocturno for piano No.1

109
accel.
a tempo
p
112
ad lib.
A Tempo I. Moderato espressivo
115
f
f
tr
tr
mf
3
6
6
3
A Tempo I. Andante a carezzevole
116
p
p
6
6
6
118
p
p
p
p

122
8va
8va
8va
8va
f
p
8vb
>
(♮)
>
125
ad lib.
8va
8vb
8vb
p
>
>
p
A Tempo I. Moderato espressivo
127
tr
tr
p
6
3
6
3
f
128
6
6
6
A Tempo I. Andante a carezzevole
129
8va
8va
8va
p
p
p
pp
>
>

Nocturno for piano No.1

147
152
Pesante
ff
A Tempo I.
156
7
16
p
160
Pesante
164
ff

A Tempo I.

168
171
175
Pesante
178
182
181
27 January 2017, Friday - 29 January 2017, Sunday
villa "Lina", v.Emona, Bulgaria

Nocturno for piano No.2

from the music cycle " PLAY OF THE THOUGHT "

20
A Tempo I.
sf
sf
sf
sf
A Tempo I. Molto moderato
30

Nocturno for piano No.2

51
sf
54
sf sf
57
sf
60
sf
sf
sf
61
sf
sf
65
sf
sf

Nocturno for piano No.2

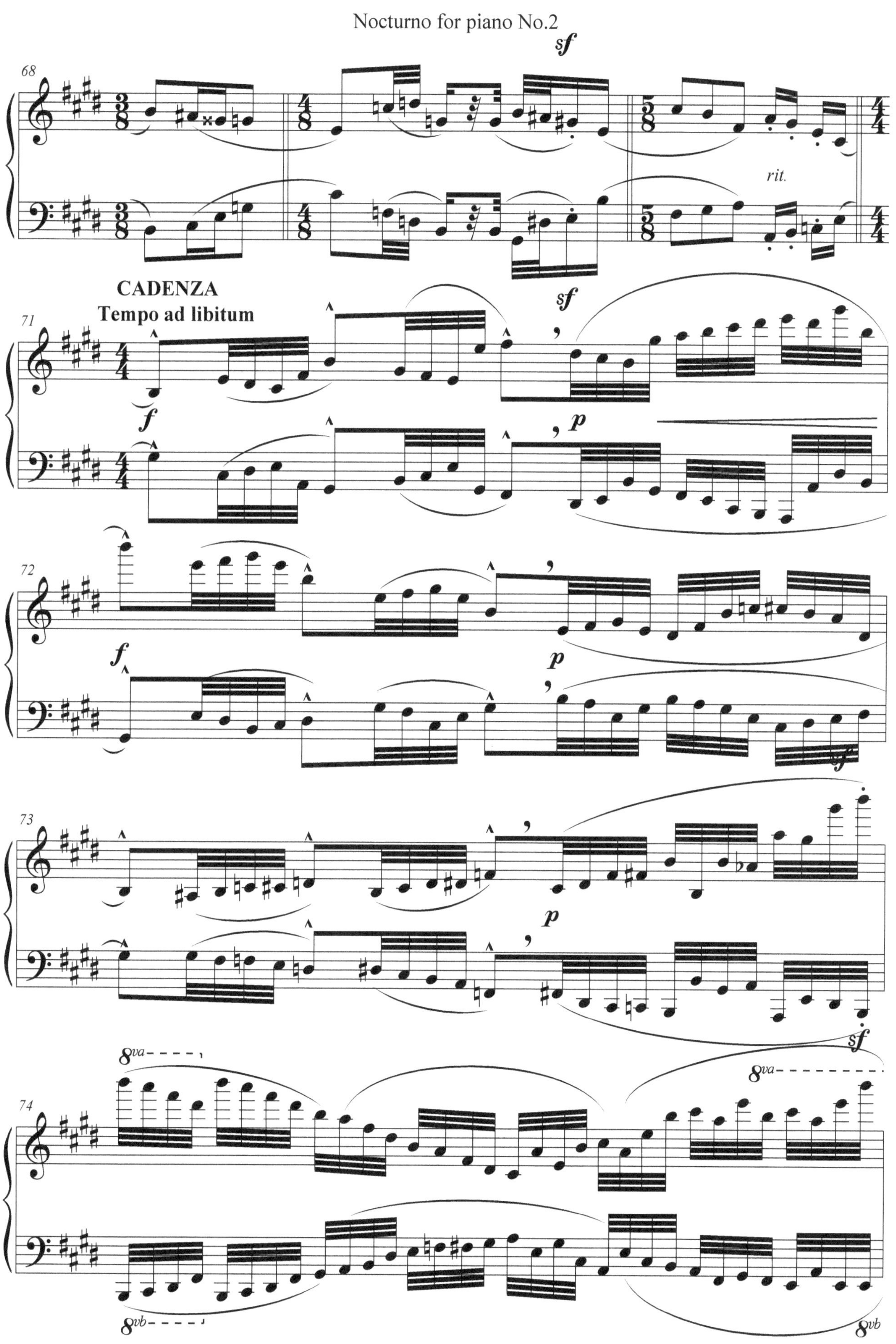

lunga
Andante cantabile con alcuna lisenza
lunga
Molto moderato
A Tempo I.
88

A Tempo I. Molto moderato
sf
sf
sf
sf
sf
sf
A Tempo I. Molto moderato

A Tempo I. Molto moderato
07 February 2017, Tuesday - 09 February 2017, Thursday
Sofia, Bulgaria